<u>UNDERTOW</u>

STORM SURGE BUILDING THROUGH THE SEA
PULLING THE POET OUT IN ME
I SHOW MY SOUL
CHEST TORN OPEN IT FALLS TO THE FLOOR WHOLE

TIDE PULLS BACK FROM THE LANDS
PULLING ME WITH IT WHILE I TRY TO GRIP THE SAND
I'M HOLDING ON WITH EVERYTHING I HAVE
BUT IT'S NOTHING TO BE HAD

UNDERTOW SLAMS ME TO THE OCEAN FLOOR
FIGHT AND FIGHT BUT IT COMES BACK FOR MORE
TRY TO TAKE A BREATH BUT IT FILLS MY LUNGS
TRY TO LISTEN BUT IT SPEAKS IN TONGUES

I DON'T UNDERSTAND WHAT IT WANTS
AM I IT'S PREY... AM I WHAT IT HUNTS?
IF I LAY MYSELF OPEN WILL IT KILL ME?
I WANT TO GIVE MYSELF BUT THIS WILL HURT
SURELY

I'VE LAID OUT AS OPEN AS I CAN
WAVE COMING OVER ME IT SEES ME AS I AM
THIS ONE LOOKS AT ME DIFFERENT
THIS DOESN'T FEEL THE SAME AS THE LAST
CURRENT

IT PULLS ME FROM THE GROUND
FILLS MY LUNGS WITH AIR ABOUND
PLEASE DON'T KILL ME I WHISPER TO THE MIST
BUT IF I DIE I HOPE IT'S IN YOUR GRIPS

PAINT THE TOWN

YOU METHODICALLY CANVAS YOUR EMOTIONS WITH
INVISIBLE PAINT
HOPING THAT IF NO COLORS ARE LEFT BEHIND IT
CAN'T SHOW THE PAIN

BUT I'M ABLE TO SEE THE PAIN YOU TRY SO
DESPERATELY TO HIDE
I WAS MEANT TO SEE IT NOW MATTER HOW HARD
YOU TRIED

I KNOW THE THINGS YOU HIDE AS THEY'RE HIDDEN
ALSO IN ME
I USED TO WEAR MINE OPENLY, NOW I WEAR LONG
SLEEVE

TODAY, PEOPLE ARE DESENSITIZED AND NOT KIND
TO GENTLE BROKEN SOULS
ALWAYS LEFT DISCARDED TO SLOWLY DRIFT INTO
THE ABYSS OF BLACK HOLES

BUT ONCE IN A WHILE ANOTHER LIFE HAS BEEN
DISCARDED AT THE SAME TIME
YOU'RE ABLE TO LINK, SWING FOR LIFE, GRAB HOLD,
AND START TO CLIMB

I BELIEVE I KNOW THE REASON WHY TO ME YOU
WERE SENT

IF I'M RIGHT YOU'LL TASTE ON ME COFFEE BUT NO
DISAPPOINTMENT

AND WE CAN TASTE OF DISAPPOINTMENT
TOGETHER WITH NO RESTRAINTS
AND WE CAN TASTE OF COFFEE TOGETHER AND
PAINT THE TOWN IN INVISIBLE PAINTS

WON'T YOU PLEASE COME CLIMB ABOVE THE ABYSS
AND PAINT WITH ME?
LET'S PAINT OUR BODIES AND COME TOGETHER AS
A VIBRANT MASTERPIECE

MAMIHLAPINATAPAI

IF THERE WAS EVER A DEFINITION FOR YOU AND I...
I'M PRETTY SURE IT WOULD BE MAMIHLAPINATAPAI

A LOOK WITHOUT WORDS SHARED BY TWO
LOOK OF BURNING DESIRE BUT ONLY A PREVIEW

BOTH WANT THE SAME BUT APPREHENSIVE
TROUBLED PASTS MAKES US DEFENSIVE

WISHING THE OTHER INITIATES
DESIRE AND PASSION ACCUMULATES

I CAN HEAR YOUR HEART BEAT LOUDER
MINE'S BEING PACKED WITH GUNPOWDER

IT'S BEEN PACKED, PRESSED, READY TO EXPLODE
IF IT DOESN'T SOON... IT'LL SURELY IMPLODE

I SEE THE LOOK UPON ME YOU BESTOW
I WAS LUCKY ENOUGH TO CAPTURE IT IN PHOTO

A LOOK WITHOUT WORDS SHARED BY TWO...
MAMIHLAPINATAPAI... NOT JUST ME NOT JUST YOU

<u>TALKS</u>

MIDDLE OF THE DAY,
CAN'T SHAKE THE THOUGHT OF YOU
MOONLIGHT SHIMMERS
ARE YOU LOOKING TOO?

FALLING DEEPER
ARE YOU FEELING IT
THE TOUCH ON MY BARE SKIN SAYS YOU DO
I JUST WANT TO GET WITH IT

WHISPERS THROUGH THE PHONE
WE ANSWER THE CALLS
IT'S ALL BULLSHIT
BUT WE APPEASE THE TALKS OF WALLS

THEY DON'T KNOW I'VE FALLEN
THEY DON'T KNOW YOU HAVE TOO
YOU HAVEN'T EVEN TOLD ME
BUT I KNOW IT'S IN YOU

DEEP IN THERE NERVOUS TO COME OUT
BUT I'M AFRAID THEY'VE SCARED YOU AWAY
I HOPE NOT....
I BEG.... PLEASE STAY......

<u>MY CHURCH</u>

MY CHURCH I SEEK HAS NO DOORS,
IT HAS NOT A SINGLE STEEPLE,
SHE HAS HER ARMS WIDE OPEN,
TO PROTECT ME FROM PEOPLE.

MY CHURCH IS A QUIET SMILE,
A GENTLE TOUCH,
MY CHURCH HAS THE BLUEST EYES,
THAT I LOVE SO MUCH.

MY CHURCH HAS NO PASTOR,
NO PEWS TO SIT,
MY CHURCH HAS NO CHOIR,
BUT IN IT I FIT.

MY CHURCH IS AGAINST HER CHEST,
FEELING THE HEAT OF HER SKIN,
MY CHURCH IS SWEET AND TENDER,
A GIFT I'LL NEVER KNOW AGAIN.

MY CHURCH HAS NO LECTURES,
NO SUNDAY MASS,
MY CHURCH SPEAKS WHERE ONLY I CAN HEAR,
SHE'S MINE ALAS.

MY CHURCH LOVES ME FOR WHO I AM,
SHE SEES WHAT NO ONE ELSE CAN,

MY CHURCH SEES THE BEAUTY,
OF WHO I TRULY AM.

MY CHURCH HAS NO JUDGEMENT,
IT HAS NO BOOKS,
MY CHURCH IS ALL FOR ME,
IT WAS HIDDEN DEEP IN THE NOOKS.

MY CHURCH HOLDS ME TIGHT,
SHE BRINGS ME PEACE,
MY CHURCH GIVES ME LIFE,
SHE MAKES ME.... ME

COMING HOME

MY HANDS, CUT UP AND ROUGH FROM A DAYS WORK
MY FACE, DIRTY, WITH A STRIPE ON MY FOREHEAD
FROM THE SUNBURN,
MY BANDANA FULL OF SWEAT,
MY TANK TOP SOAKING WET

DAY BY DAY SAME THING
DIRT TRAPPED UNDER MY WEDDING RING
MY HARD HAT BEATEN AND BATTERED
BUT WHEN I GET TO YOU IT DOESN'T MATTER

COME HOME BOOTS MUDDY
COULDN'T CARE LESS ABOUT MY BUDDIES
THEY'RE NOT WAITING FOR ME
YOU ARE THOUGH AND IT'S CLEAR TO SEE

I'M UP AND GONE WITH THE SUN
COFFEE IN STOW, POCKET WITH MY GUN
KEEPS ME SAFE TO GET HOME TO YOU
YOU ALREADY KNOW, NOTHING NEW

A KISS GOODBYE TO HOLD US OVER TO THE NIGHT
IT'S NEVER ENOUGH BUT WE MAKE IT ALRIGHT
MESSAGES AND CALLS ALL DAY LONG
IT'S ALL I GOT, MINUS WHEN I SEND YOUR SONGS

COME HOME AND I GET TO TASTE YOU AGAIN
NOT SURE HOW LONG IT'S BEEN
THOSE ARMS OPEN WAITING FOR ME
HERE I COME I'M COMING HOME BABY

DAY AFTER DAY I SEE THIS IN MY HEAD
BUT EVERY NIGHT I LAY ALONE IN OUR BED
WAITING FOR OUR TURN
FEEL THE PANIC, LOVE THE BURN

BURNING MY INSIDES WITH DESIRE
WE GOT THIS, IT'S JUST TAKING US TO THE WIRE
BUT I'VE GOT YOU THROUGH IT ALL
TRUST ME BABY I WON'T LET YOU FALL.

JUST YOU

STOLEN SIDE EYES WITH A SMIRKY SMILE
FOR YOU IT'S WORTH THE EXTRA MILE
I ASK, "WHAT'S THAT SMILE FOR?"
"JUST YOU".... BUT YOU SAY NOTHING MORE.

JUST YOU.... SITTING WATCHING TV
JUST YOU... I SEE YOU LOOKING AT ME
JUST YOU.... OBLIVIOUS TO HOW BEAUTIFUL YOU
ARE
JUST YOU... GOT ME WISHING ON A SHOOTING STAR

YOU CATCH ME LOOKING OVER MY GLASSES RIM
I LOOK AWAY TO HIDE THOUGHTS OF SIN
I TELL YOU THAT YOU'RE AS BEAUTIFUL AS EVER
YOU HIT ME WITH THAT WORD I HATE... WHATEVER

YOU DON'T SEE IT OR KNOW IT
I'M TRYING TO SHOW YOU AND NOT BLOW IT
BUT I SEE STRAIGHT THROUGH
AND WHILE YOU LOOK AT ME... YOU SAY IT'S "JUST
YOU"

I DON'T KNOW WHAT YOU SEE
WHEN YOU SAY "JUST YOU" TO ME
BUT MY JUST YOU
CONSISTS OF EVERY BEAUTIFUL THING ABOUT YOU

I WISH

I WISHED I COULD LIVE IN PLACES OF YOU
A PLACE NO ONE HAS BEEN TO
A PLACE NO DARKNESS HAS TOUCHED
A PLACE THAT STILL HAS TRUST

I WISHED I COULD LIVE IN PLACES OF YOU
A PLACE THEY DIDN'T DARE TO VIEW
A PLACE IN YOUR HEART MAYBE?
IS THERE ROOM THERE FOR ME?

A PLACE JUST FOR ME AND NO ONE ELSE?
PLEASE...I BEG.... TAKE ME FROM THE SHELF
LET ME WAKE IN YOUR EYES
ALLOW ME A NIGHT WITH NO GOODBYES....

I WISHED I COULD LIVE IN PLACES OF YOU
INSIDE OF YOU AS IN ME YOU DO
OH HOW I WISHED I COULD LIVE IN PLACES OF YOU....
OH HOW I WISH THIS WISH COMES TRUE

<u>HOW</u>

HOW DO YOU SHOW SOMEONE BEAUTY IN WHAT
THEY'VE NEVER KNOWN?
HOW DO YOU PROVE IT WHEN DIFFERENT'S ALL
THEY'VE EVER BEEN SHOWN?

THEY RECOGNIZE YOU'RE NOT LIKE THE REST THAT
HAVE COME BEFORE
BUT UNTRUTHS STILL SHAKE THEM TO THE CORE

WAS THAT FEAR IN YOUR EYES AS SOMEONE NEW
TRIED TO GETS CLOSE?
I WISH I COULD MEET THE MAN THAT DID THAT AND
GIVE HIM HIS OWN DOSE

WHAT FEAR WAS WAS UNLOCKED THAT MADE YOU
TURN AND RUN
FROM SOMEONE WHO ONLY WANTS FOR YOU TO
SHOW UP WHEN YOU'RE SUPPOSED TO COME

SOMEONE WHO ONLY WANTS TO SPEND A LITTLE
TIME
SOMEONE WHO WANTS IN CLOSED DOORS TO BE
CALLED MINE

HOW DO YOU TELL SOMEONE THEY'RE ABSOLUTELY
AMAZING
WITHOUT THEM BELIEVING YOU'RE ONLY JUST

DESPERATELY CRAVING

HOW DO YOU ASK THEM TO GIVE YOU JUST A SINGLE
CHANCE?
HOW DO YOU TELL THEM THAT LOOK WASN'T JUST A
REGULAR GLANCE?

HOW DO YOU MAKE THEM BELIEVE YOU WANT
SOMETHING DIFFERENT THAN ORDINARY?
HOW DO YOU TELL THEM THAT THEIR PAST THEY
CAN BURY?

I OFFER A FRESH START SO YOU DON'T HAVE TO BE
SCARED ANYMORE
WE DON'T HAVE TO SHOW ANYTHING BEHIND OUR
CLOSED DOORS

I PROMISE THIS, WHAT'S FOR US IS ONLY OURS
INCLUDING THE TIME THAT WE SPEND ON OUR
PHONES FOR HOURS

I UNDERSTAND HAVING TO KEEP THIS BETWEEN THE
TWO OF US
AND I KNOW YOU KNOW, SO IN YOU I NERVOUSLY
TRUST

LET'S BE SOMETHING DIFFERENT
AND I'LL SHOW YOU SOMETHING OTHER THAN
DISAPPOINTMENT

<u>LIGHT</u>

HERE'S THOUGHTS OF SOMEONE WHO FELL IN LOVE
YOU KNOW, SOMEONE YOU DON'T WANT A PART OF
SLEEPLESS IN INDIANA FOR WEEKS
YOU AREN'T AWARE OF THE LOSS OF SLEEP

DREAMS SO VIVID PRAYING THEY DON'T END
IT'S SO LONELY WITH NO ONE ON THE OTHER END
BUT TRUTHFULLY AND HONESTLY...
FEAR TAKES OVER WHEN YOU LAUGH NERVOUSLY.

ARE YOU UNCOMFORTABLE OR UNEASY?
IS IT THE LIGHT I SEE YOU IN YOU DON'T SEE ME?
I SEE YOU IN SUMMERS SUNSET ON THE OCEAN
EVERY MAJESTIC COLOR PAINTED BY DEVOTION

YOU SEEM TO SEE ME IN MORE BLACK AND WHITE
COULD YOU EVER SEE ME IN A DIFFERENT LIGHT?
WHY DO YOU LOOK AT ME THAT WAY?
I'M BEGGING YOU TO SAY THE WORDS WE DON'T SAY

BLUE MOON

NEW MORNING ALARM GOING OFF BEDSIDE
THINKS OF YOU BEFORE OPENING HER EYES
CLIMBS INTO THE SHOWER TO WASH AWAY HER SINS
WASHED AND SCRUBBED TWICE BUT ONCE AGAIN
YOU KNOW JUST FOR GOOD MEASURE
BREATHE IN BREATHE OUT NO PRESSURE
DRY OFF WIPE THE MIRROR
REFLECTION SAYS HER TIME IS NEAR
SOCKS, UNDERWEAR, SHIRT, TIE AND DRESS PANT
SAYS A PRAYER FOR HER PLANE TO SAFELY LAND
HAIR AND MAKEUP DONE UP RIGHT
GOT BAG, KEYS, PHONE, AND TICKET FOR FLIGHT
AIRPORT SECURITY SURPRISINGLY EASY
BOARD, FLY, LAND, STEP OFF AND IT'S A LITTLE
BREEZY
BAG CHECK RENTAL CAR CHECK
CAR IN DRIVE SHE KISSES THE CROSS ON HER NECK
AN HOUR DRIVE TO GET TO YOUR DOOR
SO FUCKING NERVOUS WISHING FOR AN HOUR MORE
THERE'S AT LEAST TIME TO GET BOTH A COFFEE
OK IT'S NOW OR NEVER TIME
GET OUT, SHUT DOOR, BREATHE, AND WALK THAT
LINE
STEP AFTER STEP HER FEET GET COLDER
WHERE'S THE SIDE OF HER THAT'S BOLDER?
OK HERE GOES EVERYTHING AND NOTHING AT ONCE
FINAL ATTEMPT TO SHOW YOU'RE WHAT SHE WANTS
KNOCK ONE, KNOCK TWO, KNOCK THREE....
DOOR OPEN, LOOKING BACK AT YOU..... ME
FLOWERS IN ONE HAND MY OTHER OPEN FOR YOU

OFF TO THE BALL UNDER THIS MOON SO BLUE
TONIGHT I'M ONLY YOURS AND YOU'RE ONLY MINE
LET'S SAY THE BLUE MOON IS OUR TIME
THE NEXT CAN'T COME TOO SOON
OH COME ON COME ON BLUE MOON

THERES THIS GIRL

YOU'D THINK BY THE WAY SHE WRITES OF THE
WORLD
THAT SHE'S SEEN THE SEVEN WONDERS BUT NO
SHE JUST SAYS "YOU SEE, THERE'S THIS GIRL"

YOU'D THINK THE WAY THE REST WALKED AWAY
THAT SHE'D HAVE A HEART OF STONE BY NOW
BUT IT'S STILL SOFT MUCH TO HER DISMAY

YOU'D THINK SHE'D GIVE UP BY NOW
KNOWING SHE DOESN'T STAND A CHANCE
BUT THAT'S NOT WHAT SHE'S ABOUT

YOU'D THINK HURTING HER WOULD HURT THEM
HOWEVER, THEY DIDN'T CARE AT ALL
SOME EVEN DID IT OVER AND OVER AGAIN

YOU'D THINK THOUGH THAT IT WOULD ALL BE A
BLUR
IT WAS... BUT THEN YOU CAME ALONG
AND WELL....."YOU SEE, THERE'S THIS GIRL"

YOU'D THINK SHE WOULDN'T WRITE HER WORDS
DOWN
JUST TO BE ABLE TO TALK TO YOU
BUT HER WORDS ARE SILENCE WHEN YOU'RE
AROUND

WHY DOES SHE HAVE TO TURN TO HER POET SIDE
TO GET THOSE WORDS OUT
MAYBE SHE JUST NEEDS TO KNOW YOU'LL RIDE

A LITTLE SOMETHING TO SHOW YOU'RE
INTERESTED?
THAT'S NOT TOO MUCH TO ASK
SOMETHING... JUST SO SHE DOESN'T FEEL REJECTED

FOR YOU SHE'D FLY ACROSS THE WORLD
AND FOR ANYONE WHO ASKS HER DESTINATION
SHE'D SAY "YOU SEE, THERE'S THIS GIRL"

THE DANCE

DOES MY VOICE ECHO THROUGH THE WIND?
DOES THE THOUGHT OF ME BRING YOU CONTENT?

I'VE SEEN OUR SOULS DANCE IN THE MOONLIGHT
WALTZING SILHOUETTES NOW SEEN EVERY NIGHT

THEY ARE NOW JUST ONE SILHOUETTE
MOST BEAUTIFUL IN THE SUNSET

BUT THAT'S NOT ALL THAT MUST COMBINE
NOW OUR PAST MUST COME TO THE FRONT LINE

I WON'T HAVE YOU WITHOUT THE PAIN YOU HIDE
AS YOU WON'T HAVE ME UNTIL I'M ABLE TO CONFIDE

TRAUMA, PAIN, SADNESS, ANGER, FEARS...
THESE ARE THINGS THAT TRANSFORMED OUR YEARS

OUR DEMONS OF OUR PAST LIFE DON'T DEFINE
BUT IF WE WANT ME TO BE YOURS AND YOU MINE...

OUR DEMONS MUST BE ABLE TO DANCE TOGETHER
THEY SHOULD FLOW EASILY WITH NO PRESSURE

AND IF THEY CANNOT DANCE COMFORTABLY....
THEN NEITHER CAN WE

I DON'T LOVE YOU

AND I DON'T LOVE YOU
SO YOU CAN'T TELL ME THOSE WORDS ARE TRUE
... I'M IN LOVE WITH YOU
BECAUSE AT THE END OF THE SUN FOR THE DAY
I CAN'T REMEMBER WHAT YOU USED TO SAY
I WON'T LIE BY TELLING MY MIND
THERE'S MAGIC IN US THAT WAS LEFT BEHIND
DON'T WORRY I'LL KEEP REMINDING MY HEART
THAT I DON'T LOVE YOU AND WE BELONG APART
NO WORDS CAN BE SPOKEN THAT SAY
THAT I'M DESERVING OF YOUR LOVE EVERYDAY
SEEMS AS THOUGH NO MATTER WHAT
I'M ONE TO LOVE NOT TO BE LOVED
I'M NOT IN A PLACE WHERE I BELIEVE
THAT LOVE IS PROJECTED TO ME
STARING AT OUR PICTURES I THINK...
I DO LOVE YOU

(NOW READ IT FROM BOTTOM UP)

STAINED GLASS

I KNOW MY LOVE FLOWS AS THE RIVERS
BUT OH I WISH IT WAS MORE LIKE A STREAM
MAYBE THEN I WOULDN'T DROWN IN MY DREAMS

I WISH YOU'D SAY WHAT YOU WANNA SAY
PLEASE SAY IT BACK IT'S NO MISTAKE
JUST SAY IT, WHY WAIT?

THOSE WORDS COULD SAVE ME....
MY SAVING GRACE... MY LIFELINE....
JUST SAY YOU WANT TO BE MINE...

AND IF YOU DON'T... PLEASE SPARE MY HEART
IT'S RIDDLED WITH SPIDER WEB CRACKS
OH HOW I WISH I HAD BULLETPROOF GLASS

THEN I'D BE STRONGER FOR YOU
I WOULDN'T BE SO FRAGILE, SO BROKEN
BUT YOU SEE MY DOOR AND YOU WANT IN

BUT IF YOU TOUCH IT THE WRONG WAY
IT MAY SHATTER IN YOUR HAND
BUT YOUR DOORS CRACK TOO SO YOU UNDERSTAND

HOWEVER MINE IS GLASS AND WILL ALWAYS SHOW
BUT YOURS CAN BE LOVED BACK TO SOLID OAK
MINE WILL FOREVER SHOW ALL THE WAYS I'M BROKE

MAYBE WE CAN PAINT IT
MAYBE IF WE DECORATE THE CRACKS
YOU WON'T SEE THE STRENGTH IT LACKS

MAYBE WE CAN COMBINE OUR DOORS....
A SOLID OAK WITH ACCENTS AND EDGES OF BRASS...
NOW FRAMES A MASTERPIECE OF STAINED GLASS

FELL IN LOVE

I FELL SO IN LOVE WITH YOU OPENLY KNOWING
THIS WAS SOMETHING WE COULDN'T KEEP ONGOING

I FELL SO IN LOVE WITH YOU WHILE I WAS HEALING...
SOMETHING ABOUT YOU IRRESISTIBLY APPEALING

I HOPE YOU KNOW WHEN I LOOK AT YOU THAT WAY
I'M SAYING I HAVE EVERY INTENTION TO STAY

IT'S NOT A LOOK OF ONLY PASSIONATE DESIRE
IT'S A LOOK OF HOW DEEPLY IN YOU I ADMIRE

I ADMIRE THE SMALLEST THINGS THE MOST
TAKE THEM ALL IN AND WATCH ME OVERDOSE

WATCHING YOU WRITE JUST A LITTLE NOTE
YOU'RE SO BEAUTIFUL AND YOU DON'T EVEN KNOW

WATCHING YOU GLIDE ACROSS THE KITCHEN FLOOR
I'D GIVE ANYTHING TO BE AT YOUR DOOR

THINGS EVERYONE ELSE THOUGHT WAS NOT
ENOUGH OR TOO MUCH...
ARE JUST MORE PIECES OF YOU FOR ME THAT HAVE
BEEN UNTOUCHED

I CAN'T WAIT TO LOVE ALL OF THEM...
ALL OF YOU IN ALL THE WAYS... YOU SHOULD'VE
BEEN

MY HEART AND SOUL FELL IN LOVE WITH YOU...
BEFORE I EVEN KNEW YOUR EYES WERE MY
FAVORITE SHADE OF BLUE...

YOUR NAME

CAUGHT MYSELF WRITING YOUR NAME IN THE SAND
LETTER AFTER LETTER RELEASED BY MY HAND
AND THERE IT WAS... YOUR NAME
QUICKLY HAD TO CATCH MY MASCARA AND
FEELINGS THE SAME

MEMORIES RAN DOWN MY CHEEK
HAD TO HIDE THEM I COULDN'T LOOK WEAK
I SAW YOU DANCE IN THE SUNSET
PERFECT OUTLINE OF YOUR SILHOUETTE

I FELT YOUR ARM SLIP INTO MINE
ARM IN ARM THROUGH THE SANDS OF TIME
I SEE YOU LAUGH WITH YOUR HAIR IN THE WIND
DEEP BREATH.... BREATHE IT ALL IN

I SEE YOU ROCKIN YOUR FAVORITE TOP
DRINK IN HAND YOU SAVOR EVERY DROP
I WATCH AS YOU GLIDE AND DANCE
ELEGANCE NEVER SEEN BY THESE SANDS

I SEE YOU IN THE SAND BURYING YOUR FEET
LOOKING INTENTLY CHEST TO KNEES
ARMS CROSSED OVER PONDERING THE STRIFES
WHILE I'M ADMIRING ALL YOUR STRIDES

I SEE THE SUN BOUNCE OFF YOUR EYES SO BLUE

OBLIVIOUS THAT I'M EVEN LOOKING AT YOU
I SEE THE WARMTH OF THE SUN ON YOUR SKIN
THIS IS NOT A SIGHT I'D TRADE IN

BLINKS
MY HEART SINKS
BACK TO WRITING "YOUR NAME" IN THE SAND
WISH IT WAS YOU AT THE TIP OF MY HAND

YOUR RIDE

FUCK HOW DID YOU SUCK ME IN THIS TIME?
NEVER YOURS ALWAYS MINE
CHASING RED CARS LIKE YOURS WITH INDIANA PLATES
PRAYING IT'S YOU ON ALL THE HIGHWAYS

I SEE SO MANY...
BUT NONE YOU, COMING TO ME...
EYES PEELED FOR THE DRAWING OF THE HEART
THE ONE I DREW BEFORE YOU DROVE SO FAR

LITTLE DENT BEHIND YOUR DOOR
MUSIC UP, FOOT DOWN, PEDAL TO THE FLOOR
NSYNC KARAOKE AS LOUD AS IT GOES
HAIR BLOWING OUT THE WINDOWS

SEATBELT BEHIND YOUR BACK
LEG PROPPED UP WITH YOUR FOOT ON THE DASH
90 MILES AN HOUR GOIN NOWHERE FAST
CAN YOU LOOK BACK AT WHAT YOU'VE PASSED

WISH YOU SAW ME IN YOUR REARVIEW
WISH I COULD CATCH UP TO YOU
I WANNA LIGHT YOUR PHONE UP WITH A CALL...
JUST A LITTLE TIME... THAT'S ALL...

I WOULDN'T BE ABLE TO SAY GOODBYE
AND I DON'T KNOW WHY...
BEGGING... THIS TIME PLEASE STAY...
I HOPE YOU KNOW.... I'LL LOVE YOU EITHER WAY

<u>MAYBE IF</u>

SAVE FACE IN FRONT OF FRIENDS AND FAMILY
NO, SHE'S THIS, NOT THAT
IT'S NOT THAT WAY, IT CAN'T BE

WE MIGHT OCCASIONALLY CONVERSATE ONLINE...
IF OCCASIONALLY MEANS MORNING, DAY, AND NIGHT
AND IF IT MEANS CAN'T GET ENOUGH FACETIME

NO, I DON'T KNOW WHAT SHE'S UP TO
BUT HAVE ME SITTING IN YOUR PHONE
LOOKING AT YOU LOOKING AT ME ON MUTE

NO, I DIDN'T KNOW SHE HAD THE SAME HOODIE
FUNNY WE WORE EM ON THE SAME DAY
BUT REALLY IT'S NOT FUNNY

MAYBE IF FUNNY MEANT WHAT OUR EYES SAY
OR HOW WE HATE TO HANG UP
OR HOW IT'S HARDER TO SAY GOODBYE EVERYDAY

NO I DIDN'T KNOW THEY SPLIT...
I HEAR YOU LIE TO KEEP US QUIET
KNOWING IT'S TO EACH OTHER WE SUBMIT

WE HIDE AND SAY WE DON'T TO SAVE SOME FACE
IF HIDDEN MEANT YOU FEEL HOW I FEEL
YOU KNOW IT'S TOO LATE

WE SAY WE DON'T BUT WE BOTH DO
HIDDEN OR NOT I BELONG TO YOU

FAVORITE SONG

FAVORITE SONG BLASTING IN MY HEADPHONE
WISH YOU WERE WITH ME .. WISH YOU WERE HOME

ALWAYS MORE THAN THE OTHER CLAIMS
FAKE A SMILE TO MAKE IT THROUGH THE DAYS

FACT IS I'LL NEVER LOVE ANYONE LIKE I DID YOU
FACT OF THE MATTER IS... I STILL DO

BUT FACT IS THAT WITH YOU I RUINED MY CHANCES
YOU GIVE NO SECOND GLANCES

WHAT I WOULDN'T GIVE TO HAVE YOU NEXT TO ME
WHAT I WOULDN'T GIVE TO SPEAK FREELY

WOULD YOU LISTEN IF I GAVE YOU EVERY WORD?
I'D GIVE THEM ALL AND THEN MORE

THAT WAY AND FRIENDS DON'T PLAYING IN MY EAR
HOW DID WE PASS THROUGH ANOTHER YEAR?

FRIENDS DON'T LOOK AT FRIENDS THAT WAY
AND ONE MORE CHANCE TO STAY

SOMETHING IN THE ORANGE AND I TRIED
ALL THESE SONGS NOTHING LIKE THE MELODY IN YOUR EYES

EYES THAT I SEE FLASH IN MY DREAMS
EYES THAT ONLY HAVE EYES FOR ME

HATE THE WAY AND WHEN YOU'RE NOT HERE
IF A SONG COULD BRING YOU BACK.... YOU'D BE HERE

SOULS ENTWINED

TWO SOULS MERGED BY THE PRODUCT OF HAVOC
BOTH CUT FROM THE SAME PIECE OF FABRIC
BOTH WALKING THAT THIN WHITE THAT SEEMS
GREY LINE
NOT KNOWING THE OTHER CARRIES THE SOUL MADE
BY THE GREAT DEVINE
FEEL THE DEMONS COME TO THE FRONT TO TRY TO
DEVOUR
THE BEAUTIFULLY PERFECTED PERSON MADE
BETTER BY THE HOUR
THE DEMONS SEEM TO BE THE SAME FOR YOU AND
ME
NARCISSISM, MANIPULATION, AND HUMILIATION ALL
LEADING TO PTSD
TRIGGERS, ANXIETY, PANIC ATTACKS ALL FROM
THE PAST
BUT OUR SOULS ARE FOR THE LONG RUN, BUILT TO
LAST
OUR MINDS OF TANGLED WEBS THAT HAVE BEEN
WEAVED
SO MANY EXITS FROM THE ONES THAT MADE THEIR
OWN TO LEAVE
HEART MADE OF FRAGILE BUT BEAUTIFULLY
STAINED GLASS
BUT BECAUSE YOU'RE YOU AND I'M THE WRATH,
WE COME TOGETHER AND FORM AN
UNFORGETTABLE MURAL

SOMETHING SO UNIQUE, SO MAJESTIC, SO
INCREDIBLE
HANDS MADE TO FIT IN THE OTHERS JUST RIGHT
LACED FINGERS LED US TO STEER FROM THE PLIGHT
I TAKE YOURS, YOU TAKE MINE, NO ONE LEADS
NO ONE FOLLOWS, DOESN'T MATTER JUST WALK
WITH ME PLEASE
LET OUR MINDS WANDER TO THE MOST BEAUTIFUL
PLACES
WATCH THROUGH OUR STAINED GLASS PAINTED
FACES
THIS IS SO MUCH BETTER THAN THE OLD ROSE
COLORED GLASSES
I PRAY THIS SOUL STAYS AND NEVER PASSES
JUST ONE TO STAY AND NEVER LEAVE...
DOES IT SOUND GREEDY ASKING FOR SOMEONE JUST
FOR ME?
I KNOW MY SITUATION COULD ALWAYS WORSEN
BUT FOR THE TIME I'M GIVEN... I'M SO GLAD TO SAY
YOU'RE MY PERSON

<u>GRAINS</u>

IT'S 11:59 AND IT'S ABOUT TO BE A NEW DAY
BUT 60 SECONDS FEELS SO FAR AWAY

CLOUDS MOVING FASTER THAN THE CLOCK HANDS
TIME GOING SO SLOW I CAN COUNT THE GRAINS OF SAND

EACH GRAIN A REASON THAT I'M STILL HOLDING ON
BUT EACH ONE ANOTHER REASON AS TO WHY YOU'RE
GONE

I THINK WE WERE DESTINED TO BE BUT WE DID IT WRONG
I THINK, I THOUGHT, I WANTED, I KNOW, BUT I WAITED
TOO LONG

I THOUGHT WE HAD MORE TIME
WAITING, YES, STILL WAITING FOR OUR STARS TO ALIGN

IN CASE YOU FORGOT... WE NEVER LEFT EACH OTHER
UNCONDITIONAL.... PRETTY SURE FOREVER THAT WILL
COVER

UNCONDITIONAL PATIENCE, LOVE, UNDERSTANDING, AND
GRACE
UNCONDITIONAL MEANS THIS IS YOUR SAFE PLACE

EACH GRAIN A MEMORY FLASHES AND I SEE YOU

THE SONGS WE SING

THE ONE THAT CAME ALONG YOU NEVER EXPECTED
THE ONE THAT COMES AFTER YEARS OF BEING
REJECTED
YEARS AND YEARS OF REJECTION TO A DEAD STOP
YOU'LL HAVE TO FORGIVE ME IF I FALL TO THE DROP
I'VE NEVER KNOWN WHAT RETURNED LOVE FELT
LIKE
IN THE PAST IT WAS SILENT JUDGEMENTS OF ME IN
THE NIGHT
TRYING TO LOOK OUT TO THE FUTURE INSTEAD OF
THE PAST
I'VE ALWAYS BEEN THE ONE WITH THE EFFORT TO
MAKE IT LAST
AND THEN IN FRONT OF MY EYES IS A SOUL THAT
FEELS WORTHY
BUT WHAT MAKES THIS ONE SO DIFFERENT THAN
ANYTHING YOU'VE SEEN?
IS IT RETURNED EFFORT THAT'S NEVER BEEN
SHOWN?
I NEVER WOULD'VE STAYED IN THE PAST HAD I
KNOWN
WHY DIDN'T I KNOW THIS IS WHAT IT SHOULD'VE
BEEN LIKE ALL ALONG?
WHY DIDN'T I KNOW SOMEONE OUT THERE SHARED
THE SAME SONG?
I'VE BEEN DANCING ALONE TO A DIFFERENT SONG
THIS ENTIRE LIFE OF MINE

WHILE WATCHING THE REST OF THE WORLD DANCE
ALL ALIGNED
BUT THE CLOSER I LOOK, THEY'RE NOT ACTUALLY
TOGETHER
ITS ALL A FACADE, FOR THEM, THERE'S NO
FOREVER
THEY MAY ALL DANCE THE SAME DANCE
THEY MAY ALL SHARE THE SAME SOCIAL STANCE
BUT HOW IS IT JUST ONE SONG FOR ALL OF THESE
PEOPLE TO SHARE?
NO NO, JUST THERE'S SEVERAL FOR ME AND THE
ONE FOR WHICH I CARE
NO ONE ELSE COULD HEAR THE SOUND OF THE
SONGS WE SING
THE MASSES DON'T UNDERSTAND THERE'S MORE
THAN ONE SONG THAT'S ADDICTING
THE LIFE OF SOMEONE LIVING LIFE IN LIVING COLOR
THE LIFE OF LIVING TAKING CARE OF ONE ANOTHER
NOT SOMETHING THEY KNOW ABSOLUTELY
ANYTHING ABOUT
NO, ITS ALL ABOUT THEM, ALL ABOUT THE CLOUT
THEY WON'T SAY YOU PUT THEM ON CLOUD 25
THEY WON'T TELL YOU YOU DESERVE TO THRIVE
DIDN'T KNOW THERE WAS MORE TO LIFE THAN
FOLLOWING THE MASSES
I DIDN'T KNOW THERE WAS MORE TO SEE WITHOUT
THOSE ROSE COLORED GLASSES

HANGING ON THE EDGE

HANGING ON THE EDGE, WITH MY HEAD IN A FOG
SPINNING FROM THE TENSION
I WANT TO SPEAK ON WHAT I KEEP NEGLECTING TO
MENTION

I FEEL IT DEEP INTO THE ABYSS OF MY GUARDED
BROKEN SOUL
HANGING ON THE EDGE THIS WASN'T SOMETHING I
WAS READY FOR YOU TO KNOW

THEN I SAW THE SHIMMER IN YOUR EYES
REFLECTING THE MOONLIGHT
SOMETHING MADE ME THINK TWICE... SOMETHING
MADE IT ALRIGHT

WAS IT FEELING YOUR FLESH UNDER THE GLIDING
OF MY BLADE
AGAINST YOUR CHEST, YOUR FACE, YOUR LEGS,
EVERY PIECE OF YOU DAZED

YOU LEAVE ME HANGING ON THE EDGE OF EVERY
EMOTION EVER FELT
AND ALL OF THOSE MAKE IT WORTH EVERYTHING IN
LIFE I'VE BEEN DEALT

WAS IT THE KISS THAT I BREATHED IN THE LIFE
FROM YOU TO ME

WAS IT THAT YOU WERE EVERYTHING YOU SAID YOU
WOULD BE

WAS IT THE WAY YOU LAID YOUR HEAD ON MY
CHEST
OR WAS IT THE WAY THE LEFT MY MIND IN SUCH AN
ARRAY OF A MESS

I DON'T THINK YOU KNEW I HAD BEEN HANGING ON
THE EDGE OF LIFE
HAD YOU KNOWN YOU PROBABLY WOULDN'T HAVE
STAYED THAT NIGHT

TRY TO FORM A COHERENT SENTENCE TO TRY TO
EXPLAIN WHAT I'M FEELING
BUT I FEEL MY HEART POUNDING IN MY EARS AND
HEADS STILL REELING

HANGING ON THE EDGE CAN'T PUT WORDS
TOGETHER UNTIL OUT OF THE BLUE...
YOU PULL ME IN AND THE SOFTEST VOICE I'VE EVER
HEARD MUTTERED ACROSS MY LIPS.....I DO LOVE
YOU

THESE DAYS

THESE DAYS MEMORIES FILL ME WITH SADNESS
THESE DAYS MY MIND ISN'T RUN BY MADNESS
THESE DAYS MY VOICE CALLS OUT IN THE NIGHT
THESE DAYS MY EYES CAN'T GET YOU OUTTA SIGHT

THESE DAYS GRIEF HAS BLANKETED ME
THESE DAYS LOSS IS THE ONLY THING THAT'S
STEADY
THESE DAYS I ONLY WISH TO BE TOUCHED
MORE THAN SKIN DEEP... IS THAT ASKING TOO MUCH

THESE DAYS I JUST WANT OUR SOULS TO VIBE
THESE DAYS I JUST WANT MY DIE OR RIDE
I'D SAY RIDE OR DIE BUT TOO CLICHE
I JUST WANT TO BE LOVED THESE DAYS

THESE DAYS MY HEART MISSES WHAT I REJECTED
TOO LITTLE TOO LATE WHEN I FINALLY REFLECTED
COULDN'T BE REJECTED ONE MORE TIME
BUT NO ONE KNEW I WAS WALKING THAT LINE

TASTES LIKE COFFEE AND DISAPPOINTMENT...
FACTS
BUT THESE DAYS MY DISAPPOINTMENT IS LACKED
THESE DAYS MY COFFEE IS FOR MY ENJOYMENT
TIRED OF MAKING IT JUST FOR YOUR
DISAPPOINTMENT

THESE DAYS IF YOU DON'T LIKE MY COFFEE....
THEN I GUESS YOU'RE JUST NOT MEANT FOR ME

THESE DAYS I LONG TO ADORE SOMEONE
THESE DAYS MY TOLERANCE IS DONE

THESE DAYS I WISH YOU LOVED ME THE SAME
THESE DAYS I WANNA LOVE YOU THROUGH THE
PAIN
THESE DAYS I'M STILL SO IN LOVE WITH YOU
THESE DAYS IT'S ALL SOMETHING I WISH YOU KNEW

THESE DAYS I PRAY A LOT FOR PEACE
THESE DAYS I PRAY A LOT FOR SIGHT TO SEE
THESE DAYS I BEG TO SEE THE TRUTH IN ALL
AND I BEG YOU TO TEAR DOWN MY WALL

LOVE AND MISS YOU ALL OF THE DAMN TIME
EVERY MINUTE, EVERY SECOND, YOU'RE STILL MINE

<u>ONCE MORE TO TWICE</u>

TWICE I GOT TO FEEL WHAT HOME FELT LIKE
TWICE I FELT THE PERSON THAT COMPLETED MY
LIFE
TWICE I GOT TO FEEL THE GENTLENESS OF YOU
TWICE I FELT LIKE I WAS FINALLY BEING RESCUED

TWICE I GOT TO TOUCH YOUR SKIN
BUT ONCE WAS ALL IT TOOK TO SUCK ME IN
JUST TOOK ONE TIME OF CAPTURING YOUR SCENT
JUST ONE HUG I KNEW YOU WERE HEAVEN SENT

JUST ONE LAUGH THROUGH THE MIDNIGHT HOURS
ONE TALK OF YOURS, MINE, AND OURS
ONE DRINK, ONE LOOK, ONE SHARED TOKE
ONE NIGHT TOOK US HIGHER THAN THAN OUR
SMOKE

THAT ONE NIGHT MEANT MORE TO ME
THAN I'LL EVER ALLOW YOU TO SEE
THAT NIGHT FOLLOWED BY THE NEXT ONE
THEN WATCHING YOU DRIVE OFF INTO THE DAWN

VIDEO CHAT ALL THE WAY HOME...
THEN EVERYDAY EVEN WHEN WE WEREN'T ALONE
IT ONLY TOOK ONE DAY TO KNOW
THAT I WOULDN'T BE ABLE LEAVE YOU ALONE

YOU ARE THE ANSWER TO EVERY QUESTION
TWICE I FELT YOU WERE WORTH EVERY HARD
LESSON
TWICE I FELT I WAS WHERE I NEEDED TO BE
TWICE IT FELT LIKE GENUINE FEELINGS JUST FOR
ME

TWICE I FELT LIKE I DIDN'T WANT TO LET GO
TWICE... MY WHOLE LIFE OF EVERYONE I'VE KNOWN
APPARENTLY THAT'S ALL IT TOOK
NOW YOU HAVE ME WRITING AN ENTIRE BOOK...

TWICE THERE SHOULD'VE BEEN MORE
TWICE MORE PASSION THAN EVER BEFORE

TWICE I GOT TO FEEL WHAT SANITY FELT LIKE
TWICE IS ALL IT TOOK I'LL WORSHIP ALL OF YOU
RIGHT

ONE LOOK AND I KNEW I LOVED YOU
FIRST TOUCH THOUGH I KNEW I NEEDED YOU
ANY PIECE YOU WERE WILLING TO GIVE
EVERY PIECE HELD AS A REASON TO LIVE

GIVE ME ONCE MORE TO TWICE TO MAKE IT THREE
ONCE MORE, I'LL SHOW YOU THE BEST OF ME
ONCE MORE, I'LL GIVE YOU ALL YOU DESIRE
ONCE MORE, I'LL SHOW YOU PASSION WITH FIRE

<u>BLUE</u>

A LOT OF PEOPLE'S FAVORITE COLOR IS BLUE
BLUE LIKE THE SKY OR THE SEA
ALL SO GENERIC.... MY FAVORITE IS YOU

MY FAVORITE SHADE OF BLUE
IS EVERY SHADE OF PERPLEXITY OF YOUR EYES
THE BLUE YOU TRY NOT TO LET ME SEE THROUGH

THAT INDIANA SHIRT WITH THE ZIGZAGS INSIDE
MAKES ME THINK YOU'RE THINKING OF ME
ENDLESS WRITING MATERIAL YOU PROVIDE

THINK OF THAT BLUE FOOFY IN YOUR SHOWER
IT GETS TO TOUCH ALL OF YOU...
WISH I HAD THAT MUCH POWER

THERE'S THE COLOR OF MY FAVORITE JEANS ON
YOU
THE HIGH-RISE YOU WEAR WITH THE BOOTS
EVERYTHING TOUCHED BY YOU IS MY FAVORITE
BLUE

YOU KNOW HOW TO CAPTURE ME WITH THE BLUES...
BRACELETS, NECKLACES, HAIR, RINGS, CLOTHES,
EVEN AS FAR AS THE TATTOOS

THAT TURQUOISE NECKLACE ACROSS YOUR CHEST
FAVORITE ACCESSORY NEXT TO THE MATCHING
RING
AND EARRINGS THAT DANGLE TO YOUR NECK

MY FAVORITE SHADE OF BLUE?
HIDDEN SECRETLY IN THAT OAKLEY HOODIE
THE MATCHING ONE I GOT FOR YOU

OTHERS FAVORITE COLOR MAY JUST BE BLUE...
BUT THEY HAVE NO IDEA....
EVERY SHADE'S PERFECTED BY THE TOUCH OF YOU

THE BLUE YOU GET DONE ON YOUR NAILS
THE ONES THAT SHOULD BE IN MY BACK...
I COULD GIVE YOU ALL THE DETAILS

THE MOST PERFECT SHADE OF BLUE?
THE BLUE YOUR EYES ARE WHEN YOU LAUGH
AT ALL THE LITTLE THINGS I TELL YOU I LOVE
ABOUT YOU

OTHERS FAVORITE COLOR MAY BE BLUE
BUT THEY DON'T HAVE THE CAPACITY
TO LOVE THE COMPLEX SHADES OF YOU

<u>TELL YOU</u>

I SAY I KNOW WE COULD NEVER BE TOGETHER
BUT I WOULD GIVE ANYTHING...
TO FEEL YOUR CHEST AGAINST MY LEATHER

TO GRAB YOUR LEG WITH MY CLUTCH HAND
SLIDE IT UP PAST THE KNEE
I'M SORRY I KNOW I WAS UNPLANNED

I CAME BARGING IN WITH NO WARNING SIGNS
NOTHING OTHER THAN A NAME
BUT WE KNOW THAT'S NOT WHAT DEFINES

THEY DIDN'T TELL YOU HOW I LAUGH OUT LOUD
HOW I LIKE MY COFFEE
OR THAT MY HEAD'S IN A CLOUD

THEY DIDN'T TELL YOU WHEN I GO TO BED
I ONLY THINK OF YOU THERE
AND EVERY MOMENT WE'VE SHARED

AND I KNOW WE CAN'T BE TOGETHER THAT WAY
BUT THE HEART WANTS WHAT IT WANTS
AND IT WANTS YOU EVERYDAY

THEY WON'T TELL YOU THAT'S MY HEART ON MY
SLEEVE
NO OF COURSE NOT WHY WOULD THEY

THEY DON'T WANT YOU TO SEE ME

THEY DIDN'T TELL YOU LONELINESS KNOWS MY
NAME
WELL SHE KNOWS ME WELL
BETTER THAN ANY OLD FLAME

SHE KEEPS ME COMPANY KEEPS ME SANE
WHEN EVERYONE ELSE DISAPPEARS
SHE'S THE KEEPER OF THE PAIN

THEY WON'T TELL YOU SADNESS IS IN MY HEART
I GUESS IT'S NOT SHOWN
I TRY TO KEEP TO MYSELF THAT PART

I SAY I KNOW WE CAN'T BE ONE
I TRY TO KEEP YOU AT DISTANCE
BUT TO MY HOME YOU SHOULD COME

AND THEY WON'T TELL YOU I LOVE YOU
I'LL KEEP THAT FOR ME
BUT OH HOW I LONG TO TELL YOU

MASTER KEY

FIRST GLANCE FROM ACROSS THE STREET
SHE KNEW SHE WAS IN TROUBLE
THE WAY SHE MOVED SO ELEGANTLY
DIDN'T TAKE LONG TO BURST THAT PERSONAL BUBBLE

IN HER SPACE AND HER IN YOURS
ACCIDENTAL TOUCH THEN INTENTIONAL
THIS TRANSFORMS FOR A NEW COURSE
ONE THAT'S HIGHLY UNCONVENTIONAL

GOALS AND DREAMS ALL SEEM TO ALIGN
BUT ARE THEY WILLING TO TAKE THE STEP?
ARE THEY WILLING TO GO PAST THAT LINE?
ARE THEY WILLING TO GO PAST IT ONLY BEING A
SECRET?

THE WAY SHE LOOKS AT HER....
MY GOD YOU'D THINK SHE HUNG THE MOON
YOU'D THINK SHE PAINTED ALL THE STARS
YOU'D THINK SHE'S THE ONLY ONE SHE SAW IN THE ROOM

EYES ONLY FOR HER
THOSE EYES ARE SO WEARY
THEY CHASE AFTER YOU EVERYWHERE YOU GO
AND NIGHT AFTER NIGHT SHE CONSIDERS EVERY
THEORY

EVERYDAY SEEMS HARDER TO KEEP IT IN
YOU'VE USED YOUR KEY ON THE DOOR
IT'S THE ONLY MASTER KEY THERE'S EVER BEEN
NO ONE ELSE HAS HELD THAT KEY BEFORE

IT UNLOCKS EVERY PIECE OF HER
THE PARTS SHE BURIED DEEP DOWN
EVEN THE ONES THAT ARE JUST THROWN TOGETHER
PARTS DISCARDED FROM OTHERS ON THE GROUND

IT ALSO UNLOCKS DEADLY DESIRE
A PLACE THAT BRINGS EXCITEMENT AND PASSION
A PLACE THAT MOST PEOPLE CAN ONLY ADMIRE
BECAUSE THEY'RE ALL TALK NO ACTION

USE THAT KEY IN ANY DOOR YOU PLEASE
BUT BE GENTLE WITH THE LOCKS THEIR OLD
MAYBE ONE DAY YOU'LL SHOW YOUR KEYS
MAYBE ONE DAY YOU'LL GIVE HER ONE TO HOLD

WHEN YOU THOUGHT I WASN'T LOOKING

MONTHS GO BY AND I CONTINUE TO SEE NEW,
AS THE SECONDS PASS I SEE MORE OF YOU.
LIKE, WHEN YOU THOUGHT I WASN'T LOOKING AND I
SAW THE JOY IN YOU WHEN YOU GIVE,
I SAW YOUR WILL TO LIVE.

WHEN YOU THOUGHT I WASN'T LOOKING I SAW HOW
YOU LOOKED AT OUR PICTURES TOGETHER,
I SAW IN YOUR EYES FOREVER.
I WATCHED YOU LIGHT UP A CHILDS FACE,
I WATCHED YOU WATCHING YOUR FINGERS TRACE.

WHEN YOU THOUGHT I WASN'T LOOKING I SAW YOU
ADMIRING ME...
IN THAT MOMENT I FELT SOMETHING I NEVER
THOUGHT I'D SEE.
I FELT LOVE FROM YOU I'VE NEVER FELT BEFORE,
I FELT YOU MEAN WHEN YOU SAID I DESERVE MORE.

WHEN YOU THOUGHT I WASN'T LOOKING I SAW YOU
PICK MY HEART UP OFF THE FLOOR,
I SAW YOU TAKE IT WITH YOU OUT THE DOOR.
I SAW YOU DANCE WITH NO MUSIC ON,
I SAW YOUR PEACE AS YOU WATCHED WITH ME THE
RISE OF DAWN.

WHEN YOU THOUGHT I WASN'T LOOKING I SAW YOU
WITH GENTLE HANDS,
I SAW YOU DANCE ACROSS THE LANDS.
I SAW YOU LOVE WITH NOTHING IN RETURN,
I SAW YOU WITH PASSION BURN.

WHEN YOU THOUGHT I WASN'T LOOKING I SAW YOU
LOOKING TOO....
WHEN YOU THOUGHT I WASN'T LOOKING... WAS
WHAT MADE ME LOVE YOU....

<u>WAIT</u>

CHASING YOU DOWN
EVERY ROAD IN EVERY TOWN
SEE YOUR HAND OUT THE WINDOW MOVING WITH THE
BREEZE
CAN YOU JUST HIT THE BRAKES PLEASE?
I JUST WANT TO WRAP YOU IN MY ARMS
I JUST WANT TO SHIELD YOU FROM HARMS
A 3 SECOND HUG.... FOR OLD TIMES SAKE?
IT'S KILLING ME... THIS WAIT...
BUT FOR YOU IT'S WORTH IT EVERY DAY
EVERY. MOMENT. OF. EVERY. DAY.

SOMETHING IN YOU

THEY ALL SEE SOMETHING IN YOU
THEY'RE PRAYING YOU DON'T SEE IT TOO
THEY SEE HOW CAPABLE AND POWERFUL YOU ARE
IF YOU KNEW... NOT A SINGLE PERSON WOULD BE TO
PAR
THEY SEE YOU'RE INCREDIBLE AND QUICK WITTED
BUT YOU'RE STILL MORE THAN THEY'VE ADMITTED

HOURGLASS

CLOCK KEEPS MOVING FORWARD
BUT WHY DOES IT FEEL STILL?
LIKE NO TIME HAS PASSED
HOW IS IT POSSIBLE THIS IS GOD'S WILL?

I WISH HE COULD MAKE ME SOMETHING I COULD SEE
AH YES, AN HOURGLASS!
I COULD SEE IT GRAIN FOR GRAIN
AND TRULY SEE THAT TIME'S PASSED.

I COULD AT LEAST PUT IT IN PERSPECTIVE
BUT RIGHT NOW IT'S LIKE RESTRICTED INFORMATION
NO ONE SEEMS TO KNOW
AND TIME'S JUST DRIVING BY WITH NO END LOCATION

AN HOURGLASS,
TO WATCH THE SAND FALL
WOULD MEAN TO KNOW AN END
BUT INSTEAD WE'RE AWAITING A CALL

OUR LIVES ON HOLD
FOR WHO KNOWS HOW LONG
BUT YOU HELD ON FOR ME
NOW IT'S MY TURN TO SHOW WHERE YOU BELONG

I LOVE YOU IN WAYS I NEVER THOUGHT POSSIBLE
MY LOVER, SOULMATE, BEST FRIEND,
I'M HERE FOREVER AND ALWAYS
RIDE OR DIE TILL THE END

I MISS

I MISS BEING TOUCHED DEEPER THAN THE SKIN
WHERE YOU HOLD TIGHT AND LET GO WITHIN
I MISS FEELING A HUG FROM BEHIND
ONE THAT SPINS YOU AROUND AND YOUR SOULS ALIGN
I MISS THE CARESS OF A FACE
I MISS THE WAY A PERSON WAS MY FAVORITE PLACE
I HATE THE WAY OTHER PEOPLE MAKE ME FEEL
CHEAP, INVALUABLE, NERVOUS, AND IT'S UNREAL
THE THOUGHT OF A STRANGERS HANDS ON ME
MAKES ME DISGUSTED AND QUEEZY
WHAT HAPPENED TO MAKE ME THIS WAY?
DO YOU THINK IT'LL PASS SOMEDAY?
BEFORE THIS I DIDN'T KNOW WHAT TENDERNESS WAS
I SEE THAT'S LOVE
AND NOW I MISS EVERYTHING I'VE BEEN DEPRIVED OF
I DIDN'T REALIZE TOUCH WAS MY LANGUAGE OF LOVE
MY BODY IS SO TENSE
EVERYTHING'S SO DIFFERENT
WHAT I WOULDN'T GIVE TO FEEL HANDS FIRMLY ON MY
BACK
THEN ALL OVER RUNNING DEEPER THAN PROZAC
RELEASING TENSION HEAD TO TOE
BUT NOT IN THE WAY YOU THINK YOU KNOW
I JUST WANT TO FEEL SOMETHING TRUE
I JUST WANT TO FEEL YOU

MISTAKEN

I WAS MISTAKEN IN THINKING I LIVED IN YOUR
HEART AS YOU DO MINE
I THOUGHT I RAN THROUGH YOUR VEINS
I THOUGHT YOU WANTED MY TIME
BUT I WAS A FOOL THINKING YOU FELT THE SAME

I TRY TO SPEAK TO YOU
BUT I TASTE THE BLOOD THAT SPILLS FROM MY
MOUTH
IT'S OK, IT'S JUST FROM MY HEART BURSTING
TRYING TO GET TO YOU
ONLY FOR YOU TO MAKE ME SWALLOW IT AND
WATCH ME DROWN

MY HEART SAYS LET ME LOVE YOU
BUT MY MIND TELLS ME YOU'RE OK WITHOUT ME
BUT EVEN JUST A LITTLE WILL DO
EVEN IF I'M NOT YOUR EVERYTHING

BECAUSE WHEN'S THE LAST TIME YOU SHOWED UP
TO SEE ME?
WHILE I DO IT ALMOST EVERYDAY
AND THE LAST TIME YOU ACTUALLY AVOIDED ME
AND THAT LET ME KNOW YOU WERE OKAY

YOU'RE OK WITH FAKE SMILES
YOUR SILENCE SAYS YOU'RE OK WITH ME BEING
IGNORED
YOU'RE OK WITH ME GOING MILES
FOR YOU TO NOT EVEN MEET ME AT THE DOOR

EVEN ON MY WORST DAYS I ONLY WANT TO TALK TO
YOU
TWO GENTLE LOVERS HEARTS
I THOUGHT YOU SAW IT TOO
BUT IT'S ONLY MINE THAT DOESN'T WANT US APART

I WON'T BEG FOR YOU ANYMORE
I ONLY WANT A LITTLE OF YOUR TIME
AND YET YOU MAKE ME REGRET EVERYDAY A
LITTLE MORE
THE WAY YOU TAKE ALL OF MINE

ALAS I BREATHE YOU IN MY LUNGS INTO ALL IT'S
PORES
STUCK IN THIS STILL, ALWAYS MINE, NEVER YOURS

POISON

SHE DOESN'T KNOW SHE'S POISON
INJECTED INTO MY VEINS
SHE'S A DRUG I WISH I'D FOUND SOONER
I'D GLADLY DIE IN HER GRIPPED REIGNS

SHE DOESN'T KNOW SHE'S DANGEROUS
SHE DOESN'T KNOW I'D OVERDOSE
TAKING IN EVERY BREATH SHE GAVE ME
SHE DOESN'T KNOW SHE CAUSES COMATOSE

SHE DOESN'T KNOW I'M HOOKED
SO DEEP I'M ADDICTED
SHE RAN THROUGH EVERY PIECE OF ME
NO SPACE RESTRICTED

MY ENTIRE BODY RESERVED
IT'S ALL HERS
PRETTY SURE SHE KNOWS IT
I CAN HEAR HER WHISPERS

PRETTY SURE IT'S NO SECRET
THIS IS A DEATH SENTENCE
I'M WITH HER FOR LIFE
AND I'M MET WITH ZERO RESISTANCE.

<u>YOU WANT</u>

HEY YOU WITH THAT LITTLE EMOJI IN THE CLOUD
HOW'D YOU GET IN MY HEAD SO LOUD?
HEAR THAT VOICE OF YOURS FUNNY AS CAN BE
"FIX YOUR FACE" BUT THAT'S JUST ME
I KNOW YOU SECRETLY LOVE THAT FACE
AND SECRETLY YOU'RE THE ONE TO SET THE PACE
ALL FALLS IN LINE FOR WHAT YOU DESIRE
I'LL GIVE YOU IT ALL RIGHT DOWN TO THE WIRE
YOU WANT COFFEE? YOU SIT, I'LL POUR
YOU WANT MY MONEY? TAKE IT, I'LL MAKE MORE
YOU WANT WORDS? HERE THEY'RE BLACK AND
WHITE
YOU WANT MY THOUGHTS? JUST LOOK IN MY EYES
YOU WANT MY ATTENTION? WELL, YOU'VE GOT THAT
YOU WANT MY FEELINGS? CAN'T TAKE IT BACK...
YOU WANT MY LOVE? I'LL GIVE IT ALL...
YOU WANT MY SOUL? IT'S BEHIND MY WALL
BUT I ALREADY GAVE YOU THE MASTER KEY...
FIND THE HIDDEN DOOR IN THE WALL TO GET TO ME
IT'S A SHORTCUT OFFERED TO NO ONE ELSE
A SHORTCUT I DIDN'T EVEN GIVE MYSELF
SO TURN THE KEY AND COME ON IN
I'M WAITING YET AGAIN

ANCHOR

SITTING ON THIS CLOUD FEET DANGLING IN THE
ATMOSPHERE
WONT YOU COME JOIN ME UP HERE?
IT'S SUCH AN A INCREDIBLE VIEW
WOULDN'T WANT TO BE UP HERE WITH ANYONE BUT YOU
BUT YOU'RE STUCK ON THE ROOFTOPS TRYING TO CLIMB
I LOWER A LADDER BUT I DON'T KNOW IF IT'S ENOUGH THIS
TIME
I SEE THE ANCHORS THAT ARE TETHERED TO YOUR FEET
YOURS ARE MADE BY PEOPLE AWAITING YOUR DEFEAT
A LIFE SPENT APPEASING AND PUTTING OUT FIRES OF
OTHERS
ALL THE WHILE YOUR OWN NEEDS ARE MET WITH BLINDING
COVERS
I HAVE A BETTER SPOT IN THIS LIFE FOR YOU
I HAVE A FRONT ROW SEAT UP HERE WITH THE PERFECT
VIEW
YOU HAVE TO LET GO OF YOUR ANCHORS THOUGH
MINE ARE DROPPED TO THE LANDS BELOW
MAYBE JUST ONE ANCHOR DROPPED WILL BE ENOUGH TO
REACH
YOU'RE ALMOST THERE, JUST A LITTLE FURTHER, THE
HARDSHIP'S ALMOST COMPLETE
TOGETHER AT LAST UP ON CLOUD NINE
TOGETHER... NOTHING IS IMPOSSIBLE FOR YOU AND I
TOGETHER WE ARE ONE WITH THE UNIVERSE
TOGETHER WE MAKE THE LANDS DISPERSE
TOGETHER WE DROP THE ANCHORS TO THEIR GRAVE
TOGETHER OUR MINDS CAN BE SAVED
WE'LL STAND THROUGH THE TESTS OF TIME...
EVEN IF IT'S STILL ALWAYS YOURS NEVER MINE

<u>IN THE MORNING</u>

I'D MAKE THE COFFEE IN THE SUNRISE
POUR YOUR CUP JUST THE WAY YOU LIKE IT
ON THE PORCH THE SUN COMES UP IN YOUR EYES
I DON'T KNOW HOW ELSE TO DESCRIBE IT

GREENS, GRAYS, AND HEAVEN SENT BLUE
THEY'RE THE MOST BEAUTIFUL CANVAS
AND I GET TO SEE IT EVERY TIME I LOOK AT YOU
AND THEY STILL MAKE ME ANXIOUS

WE'D DO THE DISHES TOGETHER EVERY NIGHT
NOT YOUR JOB NOT MY JOB
WE TAKE TURNS YOU WASH I DRY
AND WHEN YOU CAN'T, I'LL FIX THE THINGAMABOB

I'D GIVE YOU THE THINGS IN LIFE YOU WANT
MORE IMPORTANTLY THE THINGS YOU NEED
YOUR PARTNER, YOUR LOVER, YOUR CONFIDANT
EVERYTHING YOU DESIRE I'LL BE

IN THE KITCHEN GRAB YOUR WAIST FROM BEHIND
WE'LL SLOW DANCE TO NOTHING
I'LL BE YOURS AND YOU'LL BE MINE
UNTIL THEN, I'LL KEEP QUIETLY LOVING

FAVORITE VERSION

MY FAVORITE VERSION OF HER HAS A CUP OF COFFEE
STEADY IN HER HAND
THE VERSION THAT LOOKED AT ME WITH A LOOK I COULD
UNDERSTAND

MY FAVORITE VERSION OF HER IS IN THAT HOODIE THAT
SAYS OAKLEY
THE VERSION THAT LIKED ME BEFORE EVERYTHING GOT
SO HEAVY

MY FAVORITE VERSION OF HER I HAVE CAPTURED IN A
PICTURE FRAME
THE ONE BY MY BEDSIDE THAT MAKES WAITING WORTH
THE PAIN

MY FAVORITE VERSION OF HER IS WORTH MORE THAN
JUST THE WAITING...
SHE'S THE VERSION WORTH MORE THAN EVERYTHING....

MY FAVORITE VERSION OF HER WOULD TELL ME TO FIX
MY FACE
THE VERSION BEFORE ALL THIS SPACE

MY FAVORITE VERSION OF HER SAW ME WITH AN OPEN
VIEW
MY FAVORITE VERSION OF HER.... IS NOW JUST A
PICTURE... AND IT'S YOU.

<u>WANTED</u>

YOU CAME OUT OF NOWHERE
AND THEN THERE YOU WERE
STANDING IN FRONT OF ME
BUT YOU WERE STANDING WITH HER

I WANTED TO STAND UP AND TAKE YOU BY THE
HAND
I WANTED TO TELL YOU THAT YOU SHOULD TAKE A
RIDE
I WANTED TO TELL YOU THAT YOU WERE SO
FUCKING BEAUTIFUL
INSTEAD MY VOICE DECIDED TO HIDE.

LIQUID COURAGE LED TO 3AM TALKS
I DIDN'T WANT THE NIGHT TO END
I WANTED TO DRAW YOU INTO ME
I WANTED TO LET DESIRES PULL US IN

I WANTED TO BE CLOSER
I WANTED TO TOUCH YOU DEEPER THAN YOUR SKIN
I WANTED TO FEEL WHAT YOU NEEDED
I JUST WANTED YOU TO LET ME IN

I WANTED TO FEEL YOUR BREATH
AGAINST MY LIPS AS I INHALED
I WANTED TO FEEL YOUR BODY TREMBLE
AND IN A BLINK THAT SHIP HAD SAILED

I WATCHED TAILLIGHTS BOUNCE DOWN THE ROAD
I WONDERED IF YOU WERE WATCHING TOO
I WANTED TO CALL YOU BACK....
DAMNIT I JUST WANTED TO STOP YOU

I WANTED TO CHASE YOU DOWN
I WANTED TO BEG YOU TO STAY
I WANTED YOU TO HIT THE FUCKING BRAKES
I JUST WANTED TO BE WANTED BY YOU IN THAT
WAY

ALL THE THINGS I WANTED....
WAS EVERYTHING I KNEW I COULD NEVER OBTAIN
ALL THE THINGS I WANTED....
I REALIZE WHAT I WANTED STILL REMAINS

<u>DANCE</u>

IT'S CRAZY THE WAY IT STARTS
LITTLE JOKES AND FLIRTY REMARKS
CATCH YOURSELF LOOKING A CERTAIN WAY
STOLEN GLANCES AS THEY WALK AWAY
WATCH HOW THEY MOVE ACROSS THE ROOM
WONDER HOW THEY DANCE IN THE BEDROOM
SHOULD BE OUT OF SIGHT OUT OF MIND
BUT SLOWLY YOU START TO FIND
YOU START TO THINK ABOUT THEM
WONDERING MORE ON HOW THEY BEEN
MAYBE I'LL JUST CHECK IN
SHOOT A TEXT TO EM
HEY HEY HOW'S IT GOING WHAT'S UP
AND THEY'LL REPLY WITH A LITTLE LUCK
HEY WAS THINKING OF YOU TOO
LET'S GRAB A BITE AND SEE WHAT'S NEW
GETTING NERVOUS AS I'M GETTING READY
BREATHE... IN AND OUT... SLOW AND STEADY
PULL UP, STEP OUT, SEE THEIR FACE
EACH STEP CLOSER HEARTBEATS RAISE
YOU MOVE LIKE YOU WERE MADE TO DANCE
FUCK I'M STUCK.... YOU PUT ME IN A TRANCE
BUT I'M JUST ME AND YOU'RE JUST YOU
TWO WONDERING SOULS JUST PUSHING THROUGH
MAYBE YOU'LL COME WALK ALONGSIDE
MAYBE WE'RE STRONGER WHEN HANDS ARE TIED
COULD I GIVE UP CONTROLS?
AND COULD YOU IF WE SWITCH ROLES?
FEEL MY OWN PULSE AT THOUGHT OF YOUR TOUCH
I'D LET YOU TO DO SO FUCKING MUCH
TIMES COMING FOR YOUR CHANCE
COME PROVE YOU KNOW HOW TO DANCE

FELL IN LOVE

I FELL SO IN LOVE WITH YOU OPENLY KNOWING
THIS WAS SOMETHING WE COULDN'T KEEP ONGOING

I FELL SO IN LOVE WITH YOU WHILE I WAS HEALING...
SOMETHING ABOUT YOU IRRESISTIBLY APPEALING

I HOPE YOU KNOW WHEN I LOOK AT YOU THAT WAY
I'M SAYING I HAVE EVERY INTENTION TO STAY

IT'S NOT A LOOK OF ONLY PASSIONATE DESIRE
IT'S A LOOK OF HOW DEEPLY IN YOU I ADMIRE

I ADMIRE THE SMALLEST THINGS THE MOST
TAKE THEM ALL IN AND WATCH ME OVERDOSE

WATCHING YOU WRITE JUST A LITTLE NOTE
YOU'RE SO BEAUTIFUL AND YOU DON'T EVEN KNOW

WATCHING YOU GLIDE ACROSS THE KITCHEN FLOOR
I'D GIVE ANYTHING TO BE AT YOUR DOOR

THINGS EVERYONE ELSE THOUGHT WAS NOT ENOUGH OR TOO
MUCH...
ARE JUST MORE PIECES OF YOU FOR ME THAT HAVE BEEN
UNTOUCHED

I CAN'T WAIT TO LOVE ALL OF THEM...
ALL OF YOU IN ALL THE WAYS... YOU SHOULD'VE BEEN

MY HEART AND SOUL FELL IN LOVE WITH YOU...
BEFORE I EVEN KNEW YOUR EYES WERE MY FAVORITE SHADE
OF BLUE...

<u>BURN</u>

I'M THE FIRE YOU WANNA BURN WITH
THE KIND YOU LET SMOLDER THROUGH THE NIGHT
THE KIND THAT LEAVES YOU SOAKING IN THE
BREATH

I'M NOT JUST KINDLING GIVING A FAST BURN
I'M A METHODICALLY STACKED BONFIRE
WAITING FOR YOUR RETURN

OOZING SAP NOWHERE TO GO DRIPS TO THE BASE
JUST AS MY WORDS FALL AT YOUR FEET
BUT THESE TWO ARE NOT GOING TO WASTE

THEY'RE AN ACCELERANT AND DANGEROUS
ALL USED TO GET CLOSER TO YOU
THAT'S MY SOULS PURPOSE

AS THE SAP BURN AND THE FIRE RISE
THE ORANGE GLOW FROM EMBERS
DANCE THE RUMBA IN YOUR EYES

WARMTH OF THE FLAMES SATURATING YOUR SKIN
ARE YOU READY TO FEEL THE BURN OF PASSION
YET?
I'LL GO SLOW AND STEADY JUST TELL ME WHEN

HIDE AND SEEK

LAST NIGHT WORDS WERE SPOKEN WE DON'T SPEAK
BOTH SO OPEN AND VULNERABLE TO THE OTHER
BOTH BEGGING FOR THE OTHER NOT TO SEEK

BOTH HIDING IN PLAIN SIGHT
TELLING THE OTHER THEIR WRONG
BUT DEEP DOWN WE KNOW IT'S RIGHT

YOU WERE ALWAYS GOOD AT HIDE AND SEEK
BUT LAST NIGHT I PUT UP A GOOD ROUND
I FOUND YOU... YOUR TURN TO FIND ME

LAST NIGHT I STRUGGLED TO FIND A PLACE TO HIDE
EVERYTHING WAS SO OPEN....I WAS SO OPEN
I DESPERATELY TRIED TO COVER MYSELF.... I TRIED

AND THEN THERE YOU WERE LOOKING AT ME
I FROZE... SHOULD I RUN FOR HOME BASE?
BUT WAIT WHAT'S THAT IN YOUR EYES I SEE?

LAST NIGHT YOUR EYES SAID SOMETHING NEW
I HAD TO LOOK TWICE JUST TO MAKE SURE...
I ONLY EVER WANTED TO BE LOVED BY YOU

DON'T YOU KNOW I JUST WANT TO BE LOVED BY YOU?
BUT WE HAVE TO PUT OTHERS FIRST
SO FOR THE MOMENT OUR GAME MUST CONTINUE

LAST NIGHT WE CALLED OUR GAME A TIE
I GUESS FOR THE MOMENT THAT'S OK
AT LEAST UNTIL THERE'S A TIME FOR YOU AND I.

<u>PRAY</u>

SULTRY EYES LOOKING UP AT YOUR BEAUTY
I STOLE THAT GLANCE YOU TRIED TO RETRIEVE
SORRY, YOU CAN'T HAVE THAT BACK
EVERY STOLEN GLANCE IS WITH ME IN MY MACK

I CARRY THEM WITH ME EVERYWHERE
ALONG WITH THOUGHTS OF BEING THERE
I HEAR YOU SAY "FIX YOUR FACE"
BUT FUCK YOU'VE INVADED EVERY SPACE

MY MIND THINKS THOUGHTS OF YOU AND I
DOESN'T MAKE A DIFFERENCE SOBER OR HIGH
MY EYES SEE ONLY YOU BUT YOU KNOW THIS
ONLY YOUR LIPS MINE WANT TO KISS

YOUR SCENT STILL LINGERS IN MY BREATHABLE
AIR
YOUR PRESENCE MAKES IT TO MY QUIET PRAYER
I PRAY FOR LOVE, HEALTH, LOVED ONES, AND
PEACE
I PRAY FOR HAPPINESS WITHIN ME

I PRAY TO FEEL YOUR TOUCH REPLACE
THE FEELING OF TEARS RUNNING DOWN MY FACE
I PRAY FOR YOUR SCENT TO FILL MY LUNGS
TO OPEN MY EYES TO YOU IN THE MORNING SUNS

I PRAY TO HEAR GOD SAY THAT YOU PRAY THE
SAME
I PRAY IT'S ME THAT IN THE END YOU CLAIM
I PRAY EVERY MORNING TO KISS YOU AWAKE
I PRAY FOR COFFEE AND SUNRISES ON SMITH LAKE

I PRAY FOR EVERY PIECE OF YOU
THE QUESTION IS.... ARE YOU PRAYING QUIETLY
TOO?

<u>LOCKED CHAIN</u>

STARING AT THE CLOCK IT'S NOT 11:11 IT SAYS
2:48
THE CONTROL YOU HAVE HAS ME WIDE AWAKE
OH THE THINGS I WOULD DO FOR YOU
FUNNY, IT'S THE THINGS I WOULDN'T DO THAT'S NEW
I WOULDN'T HIDE IT IF YOU ASKED FOR THE KEY
IT'S IN HELL GUARDED BY OLD VERSIONS OF ME
DID YOU KNOW YOU COULD PUT MY MIND AT EASE
OR THAT THE ONLY THING HOLDING ME BACK IS ME
DO YOU THINK YOU COULD LOOSEN THESE CHAINS?
I'VE TRIED BUT THIS FUCKING LOCK REMAINS
BREATHE SLOW PRAYING IT DOESN'T TIGHTEN
BUT RUST ON THE LINKS SINK DEEPER IN MY SKIN
I PANIC AS MY BLOOD SPILLS OUT FOR YOU
DROP BY DROP RELEASING A NEW TRUTH
YOU PAUSE...TERRIFIED OF WHAT'S COMING OUT
IN YOUR EYES TAKING OVER.... FEAR AND DOUBT
"IS THERE A REASON THESE CHAINS ARE SO THICK?
AND WHY IS THIS LOCK SO HARD TO PICK?
WHAT ARE THEY KEEPING OUT OR IS IT TO KEEP
IN?"
AND I WONDER "WHERE'VE YOU ALWAYS BEEN?"
YOU'RE THE FIRST TO LOOK AT HOW THE CHAIN IS
RAN
CAN YOU UNLOCK THIS AND REVEAL WHO I AM?
I'VE BEEN LOCKED AWAY SO LONG UNDER THESE
"JUST BREAK THESE CHAINS" I BEG AND PLEAD

I'M READY TO BE UNLOCKED HOWEVER ONLY BY YOU
ONLY YOU...I TRUST IN YOU
YOU KNOW IT'S NOT GOING TO BE EASY
THE CANCEROUS RUST DUG DEEP INTO ME
THE KNOTS IN THE CHAIN HURT THE WORST THOUGH
PLEASE BE GENTLE.... I NEED YOU TO GO SLOW
NEVER THOUGHT I'D HELP ANYONE TAKE THESE OFF
BUT YOU'RE THE FIRST THAT'S FOUGHT
DROP MY DEFENSES BUT STILL ON MY CONSCIENCE
I HOPE YOU'RE NOT JUST BEING PRETENTIOUS
I SUPPOSE ONLY TIME WILL TELL
IF YOU'RE ABLE TO CAPTURE THE KEY FROM HELL

CAN I

STILL AWAKE, STILL CAN'T SLEEP, STILL CAN'T REST,
NOT WITHOUT YOU HERE,
NOT WITHOUT SEEING YOU IN THE SUNSET
NOT WITHOUT FEELING YOU NEAR.

IT'S NOW AFTER MIDNIGHT,
IT'S NOT LOOKING GOOD,
I DON'T SEE REST IN MY SIGHT,
BUT MY INTENTIONS ARE UNDERSTOOD.

TO HAVE YOU IN MY EMBRACE,
TO FEEL YOUR BREATH ON MY SKIN,
TO SEE THAT BEAUTIFUL FACE,
TO TASTE YOU ALL OVER AGAIN.

WHO NEEDS SLEEP?
WHEN YOUR REALITY IS BETTER THAN DREAMS,
WHEN I'VE GOT YOU TO LOVE ME,
WHEN MY LOVE IS BUSTING FROM THE SEAMS.

CAN I JUST COLLAPSE INTO YOUR EYES?
CAN THEY CAPTURE ME AND KEEP MY SOUL?
CAN I SEE THEM FROM NIGHT UNTIL THE SUNRISE?
CAN THEY SWALLOW MY INNER THOUGHTS WHOLE?

I FEEL THEM REACHING FOR MORE WITH EVERY GLANCE,
THEY WANT MORE OF WHAT I'M AFRAID TO GIVE,
BUT WHEN I SEE THEM I FEEL MY SOUL DANCE,
WITH YOU I'M TRULY READY TO LIVE.

I LOVE YOU MORE EVERY DAY,
I CAN'T WAIT TO SHOW YOU IN EVERY WAY.
BECAUSE WHAT I SHOW IS MORE THAN I CAN SAY

<u>YOURS AND MINE</u>

EYES AS PURE AS THE SKY
AN ATTRACTION TOO STRONG TO DENY
AND I'M NOT YOURS AND YOU'RE NOT MINE
BUT I WANNA BE THE ONLY ONE TO TAKE YOUR
TIME

LEGS MY FINGERTIPS BEG TO RUN UP
NO MATTER THE TIME IT WON'T BE ENOUGH
AND I'M NOT YOURS AND YOU'RE NOT MINE
BUT IT'S YOU I'M HOPING IS HITTIN MY LINE

LIPS I SWEAR THAT WERE HEAVEN SENT...
WHILE MINE... TASTES LIKE COFFEE AND
DISAPPOINTMENT
AND I'M NOT YOURS AND YOU'RE NOT MINE
BUT HOW I WISH THINGS COULD ALIGN

HANDS I DESPERATELY DESIRE TO TOUCH MY FACE
INTRUSIVE THOUGHTS SO DEEP IT'S A DISGRACE
AND I'M NOT YOURS AND YOU'RE NOT MINE
BUT I PRAY FOR OUR SOULS TO INTERTWINE

A MIND SO BEAUTIFUL IT'S CAPTIVATING
A MIND THAT COULD BE AS EQUALLY DEVASTATING
AND I'M NOT YOURS BUT YOU'RE DEFINITELY MINE
BUT THE ONLY PLACE IT'S KNOWN IS IN MY MIND

SOMETHING

SHE WAKES IN THE MORNING DREADING TO OPEN HER EYES
SHE KNOWS YOU'RE NOT BY HER SIDE
DO YOU THINK IF SHE FELL FROM THE CLOUDS SHE COULD
MAKE IT TO YOU?
MIDDLE OF THE NIGHT BEGGING TO SEE YOUR EYES SO
BLUE

SOMETHING IN YOUR SOUL CALLS TO HER
SOMETHING SAYS YOU'RE MORE THAN YOU WERE
DO YOU HEAR HER PRAYERS TO THE SKY?
SHE HOPES AND PRAYS FOR YOU TO COME BY

SOMETHING IN YOUR TOUCH BURNS DESIRE
SOMETHING SAYS YOU COULD TAKE HER HIGHER
DID YOU KNOW SHE DREAMS OF YOUR KISS?
BET YOU DIDN'T, YOU DON'T KNOW HOW YOU BRING HER
BLISS

SOMETHING IN YOUR VOICE BRINGS COMFORT UNKNOWN
SOMETHING SAYS SHE HOPES YOU DON'T LEAVE HERE
ALONE
DID YOU KNOW YOU DESERVE MORE?
BET YOU DIDN'T, YOU'VE NEVER HAD SOMEONE TOUCH YOUR
CORE

SOMETHING IN YOUR MIND CAPTIVATED ME
SOMETHING SAYS I'D GIVE YOU THE MASTER KEY
DID YOU KNOW I'D GIVE IT ALL...
BET YOU DIDN'T, BUT YOU WOULD IF YOU'D ANSWER THAT
CALL.

HALLELUJAH

THE SKY TOLD THE CLOUDS TO HOLD
HOW DO YOU RESTRICT WHAT'S DESIGNED TO
UNFOLD
IT'S LIKE TURNING ON THE FAUCET AND EXPECTING
NO WATER
IT'S LIKE SAYING THE DAYS DON'T GET HOTTER

IT WAS WHISPERED TO KEEP THE STORM
BUT HOW COULD IT WITH ALREADY TAKING FORM?
IT'S BEEN ROLLING AND BUILDING PRESSURE
LET IT GO OR LET IT OUT WHAT'S THE LESSER?

NOW IT'S BUILDING LIGHTNING FRICTION
A FEELING SO PURE IT'LL CAUSE ADDICTION
AND IS THAT ANOTHER CLOUD IN THE DISTANCE?
JOIN AS ONE WITH ZERO RESISTANCE

THIS STORM WILL CAUSE MASS DEVASTATION
ONE THAT WILL RIPPLE ACROSS THE NATION
WEST COAST, EAST COAST, AND ALL BETWEEN
CATASTROPHE NEVER BEFORE SEEN

BUT LIKE ALL ELSE THEY'LL BE OK
AND THE CLOUDS MOVE THROUGH ANOTHER DAY
THEY DON'T SPEAK OF THE DESTRUCTION LEFT
BEHIND
REBUILD, MOVE FORWARD, EXIST IN THE SUNSHINE

ALL.OF.THE.TIME.

MIDWAY THROUGH THE SUNDAY
AND ALL I CAN THINK OF IS YOU LOOKING AT ME
THAT WAY.

I THINK ABOUT THAT GAZE STARING INTO MINE
ALL.OF.THE.TIME

SATURDAY EVENING MUSIC PLAYS IN MY
HEADPHONES
AND I CAN ONLY THINK OF IS THE CHILLS YOU SEND
STRAIGHT TO MY BONES.

THE WAY YOU TOUCH ME USING ONLY YOUR MIND
ALL.OF.THE.TIME

FRIDAY, I WONDER IF YOU'RE WORKING JUST TO
CATCH A GLIMPSE
CAN YOU MAKE IT MAKE SENSE?

CAN YOU RATIONALIZE IT TO MAKE IT FINE?
ALL.OF.THE.TIME?

THURSDAY, SEE THE TRAINS RUSHING BY
I REMEMBER ON THE TRACKS YOU BY MY SIDE

OH THE TRACKS WE WALK TO FIND...
ALL.OF.THE.TIME

WEDNESDAY, DRIVING DOWN THAT WINDY ROAD
REMEMBERING EVERYTHING YOU'VE TOLD.

I KNOW YOU REMEMBER RIDING IN SUMMER TIME
ALL.OF.THE.TIME

TUESDAY, DRIVING BY YOUR HOUSE REAL SLOW
I TAKE THE ALLEYWAY JUST SO YOU DON'T KNOW

EVEN THOUGH I KNOW YOU KNOW WHAT CAR IS MINE
ALL.OF.THE.TIME

MONDAY ALMOST CALL YOUR PHONE
JUST HOPING AND PRAYING YOU'RE ALONE.

EVERY DAY WONDERING AGAIN IF I'M IN YOUR MIND
BUT I'M LEARNING YOU TOO MEAN....
ALL.OF.THE.TIME.

TWIN FLAME

TWIN FLAMES
WHETHER LOVERS OR FRIENDS
ALWAYS MORE THAN THE OTHER CLAIMS
AND THERE WILL BE NO END

WHAT I MEAN WHEN I SAY ALL OF THE TIME
I MEAN WHEN I CAN'T SLEEP AT NIGHT
I MEAN WHEN I'M CROSSING THAT DOUBLE YELLOW
LINE
I MEAN WHEN THE DARK COMES TO LIGHT

I MEAN WHEN I'M POURING MY COFFEE FOR THE
MORNING
I MEAN WHEN I'M WRITING OUT MY DAY
I MEAN WHEN I'M IN CONVERSATIONS SO BORING
I MEAN WHEN I'M DRIVING AND FIND MYSELF GOING
OUT OF MY WAY

AND I'LL TELL YOU I MEAN WHEN I DREAM
WHEN I CAN'T REACH YOU
EVEN MORE WHEN YOU CAN'T STAND ME
EVEN MORE WHEN I CAN'T STAND YOU TOO

ALWAYS MORE THAN THE OTHER CLAIMS
ALL OF THE TIME.
MY TWIN FLAME.
JUST ANOTHER PERSON TO LOVE YOU BUT ALL MINE

3AM

3AM AGAIN AND YOU'RE STILL NOT HERE.
IT'S YOUR FAVORITE HOUR TO SEE THINGS CLEAR.
IT'S MIDNIGHT TRAINS FLYING BY,
IT'S LONG WALKS LEADING PARKSIDE.

IT'S CUDDLES ON THE SWING,
HEARING THE WIND CHIMES CHIME AND SING.
IT'S DANCING ON THE SIDE OF THE ROAD,
IT'S EYES MEETING, SPEAKING IN CODE.

IT'S WALKING WITH YOUR HAND IN MINE,
THROUGH THE WATERS PARTING THE DIVINE.
IT'S WALKING THE TRAILS AND GOING ABOVE THE PATH,
DO YOU REMEMBER THAT?

IT'S SWINGING THROUGH THE NIGHT,
JUST TO SEE YOU BEFORE LIGHT.
IT'S NOT WANTING SLEEP,
BECAUSE I JUST WANT TO FEEL YOU NEXT TO ME.

NOW IT'S CALLING OUT TO YOU,
SCREAMING, SHOUTING, AND IT'S NOTHING NEW.
IT'S MANIFESTING YOU HERE,
EVEN WHEN THINGS AREN'T SO CLEAR.

3AM AGAIN AND STILL THE SAME,
WISH YOU WERE HERE INSTEAD OF THE RAIN.

<u>LOVE YOU MORE</u>

SOFT KISSES SAY I LOVE YOU MORE,
AND I CAN TELL YOU THE REASONS WHY FOR.

STILL HAVE THIS FUCKING CHAT OPEN ON MY
SCREEN,
STILL STARING AT YOUR NAME STARING BACK AT
ME.

STILL HOPING YOU HAVE CORE MEMORIES,
STILL HOPING YOU FEEL MY BREEZE.

STILL HOPING YOU SHOW UP AT MY BEDROOM DOOR,
HOPING AND PRAYING YOU'RE GOING TO CLIMB IN
AND SAY NO, I LOVE YOU MORE.

STILL HOPING TO FEEL YOUR ARMS WRAP AROUND
ME AND PULL ME IN,
DO YOU HEAR ME CALLING AND WISHING YOU ARE
WHERE I'VE BEEN?

DO YOU HEAR ME CALLING AND CALLING?
PLEASE DON'T LEAVE ME CALLING.

LOST SOULS SAY I LOVE YOU MORE
EVERYDAY... LOVE YOU MORE.

FEEL

I HEAR YOUR WORDS,
BUT YOU HAVEN'T EVEN SPOKE,
SUCH SIMILAR WORLDS,
BUT LIFELINES REVOKED.

I HEAR YOUR EVERY THOUGHT,
BUT YOU WON'T SHARE,
YOU DON'T KNOW HOW HARD I'VE FOUGHT,
HOW MUCH I CARE.

I FEEL YOUR UNCRIED TEARS,
BUT YOU WON'T LET ANYONE SEE,
BUT I CAN FEEL YOUR FEARS,
BUT YOU DON'T FEEL ME.

I SHARED SO MUCH WITH YOU,
FOR YOU TO WALK AWAY,
BUT YOU SAY IT WAS ME, NOT TRUE,
I GAVE YOU EVERY DAY.

I'VE GIVEN EVERYTHING I HOLD CLOSE TO ME...
I'VE GIVEN IT ALL TO YOU.
BECAUSE EVEN STILL YOU'RE PRIORITY,
BECAUSE I'LL NEVER UNLOVE YOU.

STILL THINKING OF YOU

STILL THINKING OF YOU
OUR CORE MEMORIES AND WHAT THEY DO
TRAINS FLYING BY
TAKING WALKS IN THE MOONLIGHT

STILL THINKING OF YOU
WAKING TO YOUR SCENT LIKE A MORNING COFFEE
BREW
ARMS WRAPPED AROUND
OUR CONTENTMENT BOUND

STILL THINKING OF YOU
ALL THE LOVE OWED NOW DUE
NO SHAME IN US
ANYTHING WE CAN DISCUSS....

STILL THINKING OF YOU
AN OLD CRUSH WITH A LOVE SO NEW
HEAR THE WIND CHIMES IN THE DARK
FEEL THE BREEZE ON THE SWINGS IN THE PARK

STILL THINKING OF YOU
THAT LATE NIGHT VIEW
AS YOU FALL ASLEEP CUDDLED UP SO TIGHT
NOT SURE HOW BUT THIS FEELS SO RIGHT

STILL THINKING OF YOU

ARE YOU THINKING OF ME TOO
I WONDER ALL DAY LONG
HOPING AND PRAYING I'M NOT WRONG.

STILL THINKING OF YOU
BECAUSE WORDS ARE NO ISSUE
MY FUTURE WIFE
YOU'VE GOT MY HEART MY SOUL AND MY LIFE

STILL THINKING OF YOU
ALWAYS YOU
TAKE YOU ANYWHERE YOU PLEASE
THESE FEELINGS CAN'T SEIZE.

STILL THINKING OF YOU
TELL ME YOU ARE TOO
TELL ME IT'S ME YOU NEED
AND I'LL TELL YOU IT'S ALWAYS GONNA BE YOU
AND ME.

STILL THINKING OF YOU
I'M SHOUTING TO THE WORLD I LOVE YOU
BUT IT'S A WHISPER IN YOUR EARS
BECAUSE YOU'RE MY WORLD FOR THE REST OF MY
YEARS.

I LOVE YOU

<u>THE DEPTHS</u>

WHEN I LOOK INTO YOUR EYES, THEY SPEAK ALL THE WORDS YOUR MIND WANTS TO SAY BUT IT'S TOO AFRAID. THEY TELL ME YOUR FEARS, YOUR HAPPINESS, YOUR LOVES... THEY ARE THE DEPTHS OF THE OCEAN, THAT HIDE SECRETS, DEMONS, AND ALL MYSTERIOUS THINGS... AND I WANT TO DROWN IN THE DEPTHS OF YOU... AND WHEN THEY SWALLOW ME WHOLE, I KNOW I'M HOME IN THEM.

<u>DREAMS</u>

MORNING LIGHT TOUCHES THE ROOFTOP,
FIRST SIPS OF COFFEE GOING DOWN SMOOTH
MORNING BIRDS SINGING AND EVERYTHING STOPS,
YOUR TOUCH ON MY FACE BEGINS TO SOOTHE.

FEEL YOUR CHEEK RUN DOWN THE SIDE OF MY FACE,
FEEL MY HEAD SINK INTO YOUR HAND,
FEEL THE WORRIES DRIFT, I'M IN THE RIGHT PLACE
WE'RE LEARNING TO UNDERSTAND.

BUT ALLOW ME IN YOUR MIND,
BUT IF WE COULD CONTROL DREAMS
I'D ALLOW YOU TO SEE IT ALL, ALL I'VE CONFINED
I'LL TAKE YOU INTO THE EXTREMES.

ALL THE WORDS I'VE NEVER BEEN ABLE TO SAY,
ALL THE WAYS I'VE SEEN YOU IN YOUR ELEMENT
SHOW YOU PARTS OF ME I'VE NEVER HAD ON
DISPLAY
SHOW YOU THE SIDES OF YOU I FREQUENT.

IF WE COULD CONTROL DREAMS,
YOU'D SEE THE MOST BEAUTIFUL OF LANDS
DEEPEST OCEANS AND WIDEST STREAMS,
THE NIAGARA FALLS IN THE MOONLIGHT AS I TAKE
YOUR HANDS

ALL OF THESE BEAUTIFUL THINGS,
YET THE MOST BEAUTIFUL OF ALL IS YOU
EYES THAT OUTSHINE EVEN THE MOST BEAUTIFUL
OF SPRINGS
A SOUL DEEPER THAN ANYTHING I CAN GET INTO.

YOU'D SEE THAT YOU'RE MY FIRST THOUGHT WHEN I
WAKE
YOU'D SEE YOU'RE MY LAST THOUGHT BEFORE I
FALL TO SLEEP
YOU'D SEE EVERYWHERE WITH ME, YOU, I TAKE
YOU'D SEE IT'S FOR YOU I WEEP.

COMING BACK TO REALITY I SIT UPON MY BED,
NOTHING IS EVER AS IT SEEMS
IT WAS ALWAYS YOU IN MY HEAD,
ALWAYS YOU THAT CONTROLLED MY DREAMS.

SAFE

ALL OF THE TIME I WATCH OVER YOU
AND NOT IN A SENSE OF JEALOUSY
BUT AS IN MY INTENTIONS ARE TRUE
THEY'RE AS REAL AS YOUR FEELINGS FOR ME

I WATCH OVER YOU IN THE NIGHT
WHEN ALL IS "QUIET" AND SERENE
BUT IT'S THEN THAT NOTHING'S RIGHT
AND WE REALIZE IT'S NOT A DREAM

I WAS SENT TO PROTECT YOU
AND YOU WERE SENT FOR ME TO SEE
THIS IS ALL SO DIFFERENT AND NEW
WILL YOU OPEN YOUR EYES AND WALK WITH ME?

I SEE THE WORRY IN YOUR OCEAN BLUE EYES
I FEEL THE PANIC SETTLE IN YOUR CHEST
BUT I BRING YOU TO BY PULLING OUR TIES
I KNOW HOW TO BRING YOU OUT THE BEST.

I'LL DO WHATEVER IT TAKES
TO ALWAYS KEEP YOU SAFE
I LOVE YOU TO THE END OF TIME
BECAUSE WE BOTH KNOW IT DOESN'T EXIST AND
EVEN THEN YOU'RE ALWAYS MINE

GREEN EYES

WERE YOU LISTENING WHEN HER VOICE CRACKED WHEN
SHE WENT TO SPEAK?
DID YOU NOTICE THE POISON BLEEDING THROUGH?
HER WORDS SPILLED OUT BUT NOT THE WORDS SHE
SEEKED
WERE YOU LOOKING TO NOTICE HER EYES SEARCHING
FOR YOU?

SOFT GREEN EYES WITH SUCH SADNESS
LOOKING UP TO YOU FROM HER CHAIR
PRAYING FOR YOU TO JUST STOP THE MADNESS
YOU CAN STOP IT, JUST LET HER BREATHE YOUR AIR

LET HER BREATHE YOU IN
LET HER TAKE A DEEP BREATH FROM YOUR SOUL
MAYBE GENTLE TOUCHES WOULD HELP YOU
COMPREHEND
THE THOUGHTS IN HER HEAD THAT TAKE CONTROL

YOU WATCHED AS SHE STOOD IN FRONT OF THE DOOR
THOSE SOFT GREEN EYES HAVE SEEN A LOT OF PAIN
MORE THAN THE HEART ON HER SLEEVE YOU SAW SHE
WORE
AND EVEN MORE THAN THE NEXT COULD SUSTAIN

BUT SHE GIVES FREELY JUST THE SAME
AND SHE SEES IN YOU
SOMETHING THAT SHE JUST CAN'T REFRAIN
SOMETHING THAT NEEDS TO BE FOLLOWED THROUGH

WHAT IS LOVE

WHAT IS LOVE
WHAT IS THE FIRST THING YOU THINK OF
IS IT THE FEELINGS THAT RUSH OVER YOU
NOPE, THAT'S QUICK TO CUT THROUGH
IT'S SOMETHING TO PROTECT
IT'S SOMETHING THAT WILL BRING YOU TO
GENUFLECT
IT'S INSTINCT
IT'S JUST REFLEX NO RESPONDING
THE GENTLE WARMTH OF THE FIRE ON YOUR FACE
CURLED UP IN YOUR FAVORITE PLACE
HOW THE SUN GENTLY KISSES THE LANDSCAPE AT
FIRST LIGHT
HOW THE OCEANS ROLL UP THE SANDS AT MIDNIGHT
IT'S ALL SO GENTLE AND BEAUTIFUL
IT'S SOMETHING THAT'S IRREFUTABLE
IT'S ALL SOMETHING I MISS
I DON'T KNOW WHY IT'S JUST WHAT IT IS.

AWAIT

I AWAIT FOR YOU TO OPEN YOURSELF TO ME
WHEN YOU TELL ME YOUR 3 AM SECRETS
WHEN YOU TELL ME YOU'RE LONELY
WHEN YOU CALL ME BECAUSE YOU'RE SLEEPLESS

I DIDN'T KNOW YOU WERE CYANIDE
SEEPING THROUGH MY SKIN
WHEN YOU TOUCHED IT THE FIRST TIME
THAT'S WHEN THE POISONING SANK IN

ATTACKED THE VISION FIRST
I COULD ONLY SEE YOU
FROM THERE IT ONLY GOT WORSE
STRANGE UNKNOWN FEELINGS ANEW

NEXT WAS MY MIND
AND THEN MY NERVOUS SYSTEM
DIDN'T EVEN REALIZE MY BODY WAS MINE
YOU SOAKED ALL OF ME IN

AND I STILL AWAIT FOR YOU TO SEE ME
SEE ME DEEPER THAN YOU CAN LOOK
IT'S SOMETHING I FORESEE
YOU'LL READ ME LIKE A BOOK

BUT WILL YOURS BE OPEN TO BE READ?
WILL YOU ALLOW ME TO READ WITH YOU?
WILL YOU WANT ME IN YOUR HEAD?
....I JUST WANNA GET TO KNOW YOU...

I WANT YOUR 3 AM SECRETS....
I WANT YOU TO CALL WHEN YOU'RE SLEEPLESS....
I DON'T WANT YOU TO BE LONELY....
I DON'T WANT YOU TO CALL ANYONE BUT ME....

FINAL CHAPTER

SO THIS IS IT
THE LAST BOOK TO BE WRIT

YOU MY LOVE WILL BE MY FINAL CHAPTER
MY HAPPY EVER AFTER

I CAN'T WAIT TO SEE YOU EVERY MORNING WHEN I WAKE
THIS MAKES IT WORTH EVERY MISTAKE

I CAN'T WAIT TO SEE YOU AT THE KITCHEN TABLE WITH
COFFEE
I SEE IT SO VIVID YOU ACROSS THE TABLE FROM ME

AND I CAN'T WAIT TO GO TO BED WITH YOU EVERY NIGHT
BUT MOST OF ALL I CAN'T WAIT TO LOVE YOU RIGHT

YOU DESERVE A LOVE WORTH THE WAIT
A LOVE THAT NO ONE CAN DICTATE

THIS IS THE BEST PART OF EVERY FAIRY TALE
NOTHING LEFT TO MAKE US DERAIL... EXHALE

WE CAN FINALLY CATCH OUR BREATH AGAIN
CHEERS TO THE REST OF OUR LIVES... AMEN

www.ingramcontent.com/pod-product-compliance
Lightning Source LLC
Chambersburg PA
CBHW031319250726
48656CB00005B/1882